THEN & NOW

BOWLING GREEN

OPPOSITE: This image of Main Street from May 1928 shows a view looking east from a window in the Potter Opera House on the corner of Main and College Streets toward the Helm Hotel at Main and State Streets. There are more than 100 automobiles visible in this view that covers a little more than one block of Main Street. During this time period, downtown Bowling Green was the hub of activity for the surrounding area. (Kentucky Library Collection, Western Kentucky University [WKU].)

THEN & NOW

BOWLING GREEN

Kevin Comer and Ben Runner Jr.

To my loving family—my wife, Tina, Danielle and Mark Helit, Elizabeth and Nicholas Wells, and my youngest, Adam—thank you for all the support and encouragement that you have provided. Thanks to my siblings, Janet, Joe, and David. I also dedicate this work to Joey Carlton Comer Jr. and Shawn Michael Porter, precious sons taken from their families too young.

—Kevin Comer

I dedicate my portion of this book to my family and to the memory of a good friend and mentor, Dean Maggard.

—Ben Runner Jr.

Copyright © 2010 by Kevin Comer and Ben Runner Jr.
ISBN 978-0-7385-6696-2

Library of Congress Control Number: 2009936034

Published by Arcadia Publishing
Charleston SC, Chicago IL, Portsmouth NH, San Francisco CA

Printed in the United States of America

For all general information contact Arcadia Publishing at:
Telephone 843-853-2070
Fax 843-853-0044
E-mail sales@arcadiapublishing.com
For customer service and orders:
Toll-Free 1-888-313-2665

Visit us on the Internet at www.arcadiapublishing.com

ON THE FRONT COVER: The Columbia Theatre became the Capitol Theatre during a 1920 remodel. In March 1939, this new Capitol Theatre opened on the same site and showed movies until 1972. Abandoned and neglected, it was given new life in 1981, when it was restored to become the Capitol Arts Center, hosting plays, concerts, and other events. Time has been good to this block, with only the Troy Laundry razed to provide access to parking through a picturesque alley. (Then, Leon Garrett photograph; now, Ben Runner Jr. photograph.)

ON THE BACK COVER: Perhaps the most photographed place in Bowling Green, Fountain Square Park has remained an iconic symbol of the city since being designed by John Cox Underwood in 1871. The first stone fountain lasted just 10 years and was replaced with a cast-iron fountain dedicated in 1882. That fountain remained until being recast in 1987. The Greek goddess Hebe crowns the fountain and statues of goddesses Pomona, Ceres, Flora, and Melpomene stand around it. (Marshall Love photograph.)

CONTENTS

ACKNOWLEDGMENTS

This project began with coauthors Kevin Comer and Ben Runner Jr. comparing old photographs of Bowling Green to recent images we had taken. After studying changes to many locations, we decided to put some of these into book form. We have made an effort to include not only popular subjects but also some less well-known places. During this project, we documented most existing structures in the downtown area, took photographs, and researched the history of homes and businesses. Several of those that we documented have already been destroyed.

Along the way, we have been fortunate to enlist the help of so many. Greg Hughes gave us access to his large postcard collection. Leon Garrett provided us with slides from the late 1940s, showing us a downtown Bowling Green that we had never seen. Thankfully Leon had preserved these images over the years. Viewing those photographs, we realized that much of Bowling Green's historic downtown area had disappeared. While some change is inevitable, it is difficult to comprehend how entire city blocks can be razed for seldom-used parking lots. As an example, during our work on this project, the Ora Porter home on College Street was razed to be replaced by a parking garage surrounded by retail development. Porter was the first registered nurse in Bowling Green—quite a feat for an African American growing up in the Victorian era. Just four years after a historical marker was erected in front of the home, all that remains is a parking lot. Marshall Love also contributed several rare images, including many of his own photographs that we would never have found otherwise. Marshall has been a wealth of information during this project, and we are very thankful.

Many other images were obtained from the Kentucky Library and Museum at Western Kentucky University. The library and staff proved invaluable for research, and the library's photograph collection is extensive. We would like to thank Nancy Baird and Jonathan Jeffrey for their special assistance.

Others to assist us were Judy Woosley, Dean Maggard, Ben Runner Sr., Mike Dowell, John Davis, Bill Hardy Jr., Thomas H. Baker, and John Phelps. We would also like to thank our editors Luke Cunningham and Amy Perryman for their support and guidance through this project. Unless otherwise noted, all "now" images appear courtesy of Ben Runner Jr.

INTRODUCTION

Warren County, Kentucky, was officially established in March 1797 by the Kentucky General Assembly. Bowling Green was established in 1798. Warren County was carved from a portion of what is now Logan County. This area of Kentucky Territory had been explored by a group of explorers called "Long Hunters" in June 1775. They left carvings of initials, names, and dates on beech trees along what was later called the Big Barren River. Later other pioneers established more permanent settlements in the area. The first of these was by Andrew McFadin on the north side of the Barren River near where present-day I-65 crosses to the east of Bowling Green.

Robert Moore was one of the settlers who paused at McFadin's Station in the early 1790s before continuing to his own homestead near a large spring at what later became Bowling Green.

In 1792, Kentucky became the 15th state, and land grants brought Revolutionary War veterans from Virginia into the area. Warren County was named in honor of Dr. Joseph Warren, a hero at the Battle of Bunker Hill. Robert Moore and his brother George donated a 2-acre plot on which to build a log courthouse and jail. This area is now Fountain Square Park. In 1798, the brothers donated 30 more acres to surround the courthouse and jail for construction of a town. At the first county commissioners meeting in early 1798, it was decided that the town "be called and known by the name of Bolin Green." Likely the town was named for Bowling Green Square in New York City, where patriots had pulled down a lead statue of King George III to make bullets used in the American Revolution. After a contest with Jeffersonville and New Hope, both settlements on the Barren River, Bowling Green won out as the county seat, designated in 1809. By that time, shops, taverns, and homes lined the streets around the courthouse and jail, and the city was becoming established as the commercial center for the area. Its population in 1810 was 154 residents.

By the late 1820s, Bowling Green had a branch of the Bank of the Commonwealth, a doctor's office, a newspaper, a private school for boys, and several churches. Stagecoach lines connected Bowling Green to Louisville, Nashville, and Hopkinsville. Flatboats transported goods on the Barren River. In the 1830s, business leaders, including James Rumsey Skiles, funded clearing of snags to improve navigation on the Barren River, and they established the Portage Railroad in 1832 from the boat landing and docks to the center of town. Shortly thereafter, they received funding from the legislature to construct a series of locks and dams on the Barren and Green Rivers, creating an important transportation link for shipments of goods via steamboat. The Louisville and Nashville Turnpike was completed in 1838 and provided an easier path on which to travel to and from the town by road.

When the Louisville and Nashville Railroad (L&N) was chartered in 1850, it was given permission to build a main line south from Louisville to the Tennessee state line in the direction of Nashville. Two main routes were being considered, with one passing through Bowling Green and the other passing through Glasgow, Kentucky. With a branch line planned to Memphis, the route through Bowling Green seemed to be the best choice. The citizens of Bowling Green did not want to leave anything to chance. They planned their own route to Nashville, raised $1 million, and subscribed to the Bowling Green and Tennessee Railroad in 1851. Glasgow was only able to raise $361,000, and the L&N selected the route through Bowling Green. Bowling Green and Tennessee Railroad stock was transferred to the L&N. A large roundhouse, shops, passenger depot, and yard facilities were constructed, and the railroad was completed in 1859. This was a major development in the town's growth.

Bowling Green had vowed to remain neutral during the Civil War but was occupied by a large force of Confederates by September 1861. They began to build fortifications on the city's high points, and Bowling Green became the Confederate capital of Kentucky. The Confederates evacuated in February 1862 and burned key structures while the Union army shelled the town from across the Barren River. Federal troops occupied the city for the balance of the war. The three decades after the Civil War were a time of growth in the city. The third county courthouse was constructed in 1868, and many of the structures around the square were built during this period. Electric streetlights appeared in 1886, and a waterworks system was developed. In 1889, mule-drawn streetcars appeared, with electric cars replacing them by 1898. Bowling Green had been mostly agricultural into the late 1800s, but some businesses, like the Carrie Taylor dressmaking facility, employed hundreds by 1906, shipping goods all over the world. The Commercial Club, predecessor to the Bowling Green Area Chamber of Commerce, was in place by the beginning of the 20th century. Other early Bowling Green industries were Scott Tobacco Company, Southern Cut Stone Company, and Turner-Day-Woolworth Axe Handle Factory.

Another event contributing greatly to Bowling Green's development was the decision of A. W. Mell and J. Tom Williams to relocate their Southern Normal School from Glasgow to Bowling Green in the 1880s. With student housing facilities lacking at the Glasgow campus, some prominent Bowling Green businessmen lured the school to Bowling Green. In 1892, as the school struggled, brothers H. H. and T. C. Cherry purchased it and gave it a rebirth. It became a state normal school in 1906. That school, now Western Kentucky University, has grown into a major campus, continuing to expand and influence Bowling Green's own growth today. Enrollment for the fall 2009 semester was more than 20,000 students, while the current Bowling Green population is around 55,000.

By 1940, the town's population had grown to 14,385, and large manufacturing plants such as Union Underwear, Detrex, and Holley Carburetor would continue to add jobs in the city over the next three decades. The 1940s also saw the construction of a bypass around Bowling Green's east side, which helped that part of the city expand. Purchased and developed into a large regional amusement park and racetrack in the 1940s by Charlie Garvin, Beech Bend Park had begun as a picnic area and dance pavilion in 1907. Today this park brings hundreds of thousands to Bowling Green. Lost River Cave hosted a nightclub in the 1940s and today is one of the major tourist attractions. By 1960, the population would nearly double to reach 28,338. By 1970, Bowling Green would pass Ashland, Paducah, and Newport in population. In 1964, Bowling Green's first mall opened, taking business away from downtown stores. An even larger mall opening in 1979 took patrons out to Scottsville Road. In 1981, the General Motors Corvette Assembly Plant moved to Bowling Green from St. Louis. This led the way for the popular National Corvette Museum, drawing thousands to the city annually.

Downtown redevelopment began with construction of Bowling Green Ballpark, bringing minor-league baseball back to the area. If plans come to fruition, the downtown area will again become a focal point, not an afterthought. Today Bowling Green is a regional hub in education, commerce, manufacturing, agriculture, and tourism. Then & Now: *Bowling Green* shows contrasting views identifying changes as the city has grown. These photographs will provide knowledge of what happened to some of Bowling Green's past.

CHAPTER 1

LANDMARKS

Bowling Green Ice and Cold Storage Company was built overlooking the boat landing in 1888 by John Robinson and E. B. Seely. In the 1920s, it produced nearly 100 tons of ice daily, some shipped via boat and rail. Razed long ago, some ruins are visible on the banks of the Barren River near the Delafield Power Plant. (Greg Hughes collection.)

The Warren County Courthouse at Tenth and College Streets was completed in 1869, replacing the courthouse in Fountain Square Park. An extensive renovation to this structure was completed in 1957. A new Warren County Justice Center was built beside the Federal Building on Center Street in the 1990s and later expanded into a majestic structure that severed Tenth Street permanently. The old courthouse serves as the home of the Warren County Sheriff's Department and Warren Fiscal Court. (Greg Hughes collection.)

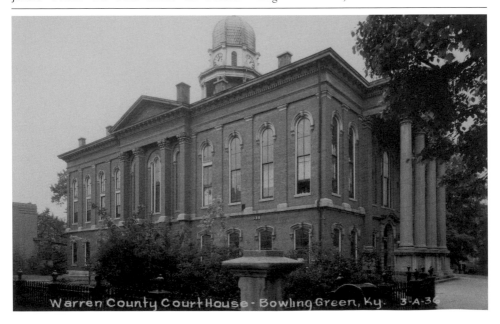

Warren County Court House - Bowling Green, Ky. 3UA-36

Bowling Green City Hall moved from the McCormack Building into this Brinton B. Davis–designed structure completed in 1907 on College Street. In 1908, the Central Fire Station was constructed behind this building. Also designed by Davis, it had matching architectural elements. The City Commission still meets in the upstairs chambers today, but the building's interior has been extensively remodeled. The four-bay fire station was razed for parking after a new fire headquarters opened on Fairview Avenue. (Greg Hughes collection.)

.S. Post Office and Court House - Bowling Green, Ky.　3-A-81

The U.S. Post Office and Federal Building at Main and Center Streets was constructed in 1912. The post office moved from the basement to the site of the razed College Street School in 1963. In the 1990s, the Federal Building was renamed to honor U.S. Representative William H. Natcher, who served from 1953 until his death in 1994. Natcher had 18,401 consecutive roll calls. The later image shows the new Warren County Justice Center in the background. (Greg Hughes collection.)

LANDMARKS

Dr. T. O. Helm acquired the old Morehead House Hotel in 1915 and later added a third floor. In January 1924, he opened the newly constructed four-story, 110-room Helm Hotel on the same site. During its heyday, this local landmark was the center of activity in Bowling Green. The Helm family sold the hotel in 1969, and it was razed in 1970. A new Citizen's National Bank opened in 1972 and is currently part of U.S. Bank. (Greg Hughes collection.)

The City-County Hospital was designed in 1925 by R. E. Turbeville and constructed on one of the city's highest points on College Hill, now known as Reservoir Hill. In 1980, the hospital moved down Park Street to the foot of the hill. Now known as the Medical Center at Bowling Green, the campus has expanded rapidly, consuming the surrounding neighborhood, the former High Street High School, and several businesses along the 31W Bypass for parking and expansion. (Marshall Love collection.)

The Louisville and Nashville Railroad Passenger Station on Kentucky Street opened in 1925, replacing an aging station a few blocks south on Adams Street. The original station was burned by retreating Confederates during the Civil War. Passenger service ended in 1979, and the station closed. On the verge of being destroyed, it was saved by rallying groups and eventually restored. Today the depot hosts many events and houses the Historic Railpark and Train Museum as well as office space. (Marshall Love collection.)

The Delafield Power Plant sits on a bluff along Barren River and began operation in July 1931. The Kentucky-Tennessee Light and Power facility housed three generators, with steam supplied by the three boilers. The plant's substation was adjacent, and a pump house on the river supplied the water. Beautiful landscaping and a stone wall surrounded the facility. Now the TVA property houses a substation, but sadly, the old plant's buildings and grounds seem neglected. (Kentucky Library Collection, WKU.)

In 1861, Confederate forces constructed fortifications on high points around Bowling Green to protect the roads, L&N Railroad, and Barren River from enemy advance. After the Confederate retreat, Union forces completed these forts. This view shows the remains of Fort C. F. Smith on College Hill, now called Reservoir Hill. Little trace of the fort remains, and the hill is known for the patriotic red, white, and blue water tank. Visible for miles, it rises 129 feet. (Greg Hughes collection.)

This wooden bridge was burned by night riders in 1915 to protest Judge H. H. Denhardt's anti-bootlegging policy. The College Street Bridge was constructed here using remains of the piers and provided a northern entry to Bowling Green. Today the bridge, minus its tollhouse, is the focal point of a riverfront park, providing pedestrians a scenic overlook of the Barren River. In the current photograph, the restored pedestrian bridge is in the foreground, with the U.S. 31W and CSX Railroad bridges in the distance. (Greg Hughes collection.)

The oldest standing brick structure in Bowling Green is the Mariah Moore House, built in 1818 by Elizabeth and George Moore. One of their five children, Mariah, never married and occupied the home until her death in 1888. Longtime home to Moseley Brothers Floor Coverings, the house was purchased in 1979 and refurbished into Mariah's 1818 restaurant. An October 1995 fire gutted the restaurant; however, much of original portion survived, and the structure was rebuilt. (Kentucky Library Collection, WKU.)

The YMCA building opened on State Street at Eleventh Street in 1909. The four-story landmark boasted a swimming pool, library, gym, offices, and 22 bedrooms. Sold and remodeled in 1931, the YMCA became the Park City Hotel, which burned in 1985. Only the coffee shop, now a pet-grooming salon, has survived from the 1949 image to the current photograph. At right, the First Christian Church occupies a structure built in 1959 after the dome slipped. (Leon Garrett photograph.)

The Mansard Hotel operated from 1892 to 1969 at the southeast corner of Main and Center Streets. Joseph Winans had purchased the building in 1891 and remodeled it into the Mansard, named for its distinctive roof. For many years, it was one of the premier hotels in the area and featured fine dining. The massive hotel burned in 1969, and a hotel employee was killed in the fire. The contrasting 1950 and current views show another landmark replaced with parking. (Leon Garrett photograph.)

Elks Lodge No. 320 had met here for more than 80 years at the time of this January 29, 1978, fire that destroyed the building. The lodge had been on the third floor, offices were on the second floor, and two storefronts occupied the ground level. It was the longtime home of Pearson's Drugs. The new Elks structure was rebuilt as a single-story building in 1981 and now houses Merrill Lynch and the law offices of Ed Faye. (Ben Runner Jr. photograph.)

The four-story McCormack Building on State Street was Bowling Green's tallest structure when it burned on July 5, 1911. The 40,000-square-foot building, erected in 1898, had housed a grocery, hardware store, bowling alley, offices, the Business University, and even city hall until 1908. Materials were salvaged, and the Price Building was erected from the ruins in 1912. This has been the longtime home of United Furniture and housed a C.D.S. Drugstore for many years. (Greg Hughes collection.)

Another Brinton B. Davis design, the 1927 Denhardt Armory on Tenth Street at Chestnut Street was occupied by the National Guard until 1965. Named for former Kentucky lieutenant governor and Bowling Green native Henry Denhardt, the three-story administration building fronted the large brick drill hall. The drill hall was rebuilt in 1947 after being destroyed by fire. The armory later housed WBKO Television studios for many years before being remodeled in 1991 as professional offices by Heritage Builders. (Kentucky Library Collection, WKU.)

The Tobias Grider home was built in 1854 and is known as "House of 10 Gables" for its unusual roof design. In 1937, this home transferred into the Paul C. Deemer family, which had a large floral business nearby. The Deemer family renovated the home, and for a long time, it was one of Bowling Green's beautiful estates. The home survives today hidden in a busy commercial district near the end of Lehman Avenue. (Kentucky Library Collection, WKU.)

Boxwood, constructed by John B. Clark in 1843 at 1234 State Street, was named for the large number of boxwoods planted on the grounds. It was purchased by prominent banker Pleasant J. Potter in 1865, later given as a gift to his daughter Sallie Willis, and finally purchased from Sallie's daughters by O. V. Clark. Other than removal of shutters and some ivy growth, there is little change visible in the views taken some 50 years apart. (Kentucky Library Collection, WKU.)

STREET SCENES

This 1912 view of Main Street from Fountain Square Park shows dirt streets, trolley tracks, and a dray for moving freight. The original trolley tracks led from the L&N Depot at Main and Adams Streets to the Morehead House Hotel, visible at left of the trees lining East Main Street. Note the awnings over the storefronts. (Greg Hughes collection.)

From the busy Main Street scene of 1948 shown in the older image, only a handful of buildings remain. The Federal Building (center), Patsy Fitzpatrick Building, and Spot Cash Store (both at right) remain today, while the left side shows five buildings now missing. The first three buildings at left, including the Avalon Hotel, were razed for parking. This previously happened to the Greyhound bus terminal in 1957 and the Mansard Hotel after it burned in 1969. (Leon Garrett photograph.)

Then and now, 1948 and 2009, is revealed in this College Street scene at Main Street. The Potter Opera House at right was built in 1866 by John Cox Underwood, as Odeon Hall. After fire gutted the interior in 1899, it was reconstructed. It has been home to Bowling Green Bank and Trust and successor bank BB&T for many years. This block has undergone a transformation from shopping and entertainment to professional offices and specialty stores. (Leon Garrett photograph.)

Before relocating, the Citizen's National Bank boasted a beautiful facade on Park Row from 1922 to 1972. Renamed the Park Row Executive Building, it burned in 1984, and the facade was razed in 1992. A BB&T bank building replaced the vacant lot in 2009. A Park Row landmark, the three-story Odd Fellows Building (center) hosted the Aeolian Lodge upstairs for over 100 years. Three buildings on the west end burned and were replaced with Park Row Apartments. (Leon Garrett photograph.)

This image from around 1930 shows the original Seth Thomas clock installed by Campbell's Jewelers in front of their business in September 1913. A Bowling Green landmark, the clock remained here until Campbell retired in the 1940s, when it was relocated down the block to American National Bank. Businesses have come and gone, but this row of buildings on State Street between Main Street and Park Row has remained mostly unchanged for many years. (Kentucky Library Collection, WKU.)

The oldest surviving building on Fountain Square is the Quigley-Younglove Building on the southeast corner of Main and State Streets. Joseph Younglove started a drugstore here in the Thomas Quigley Building in 1842, and under various ownership, a drugstore was located here continuously until 1980. A 1949 view shows longtime occupant Williams Drugs, a liquor store, and Castner-Knott. Today Barbara Stewart's Invitations on Main and Holland House Coins and Stamps occupy this corner. (Leon Garrett photograph.)

The most noticeable change visible in these views from 1948 and today is the different attitude toward signage. The older image shows multiple signs, including a large Royal Crown soda bottle on the C.D.S. Drugstore at State and Main Streets. Next door, the Barr Building, constructed around 1880, was home of Hartig and Binzel Jewelers from 1929 to the 1980s. Today the environment is much more sterile, with subtle, almost unnoticeable signage. (Greg Hughes collection.)

The three-story Getty Building at left was constructed in 1871 at 440 Main Street. It is known to most Bowling Green residents as the home of Faxon's Western Auto from 1942 to 1992. At one time, the Parakeet Restaurant occupied the left storefront. Today restaurants 440 Main and Miki's on Main occupy the first floor. Barbara Stewart Interiors has occupied the Barr Building (center) since the 1970s. Parking meters, once a downtown fixture, are no longer used. (Leon Garrett photograph.)

STREET SCENE - BOWLING GREEN, KY.

This 1940s postcard view looking north from Tenth Street on State Street shows a multitude of businesses. Notable are Hancock-Hill Furniture, Callis Drugs, Warren County Hardware, and the Mitchell Building, which housed Eugene Franklin's photography studio upstairs. Franklin took photographs in Bowling Green between 1916 and 1946. Today the original buildings between Park Row and Tenth Street are gone. National City Bank occupies the east side of State Street. The buildings on the west side were razed. (Greg Hughes collection.)

A view of State Street looking north from Eleventh Street in 1949 shows busy two-way traffic. Note the Oldsmobile dealership at right and the Chevrolet dealership further down the block, next door to the Price Building. The view in 2009 shows the former Sears Building, occupied now by State of Kentucky offices. At left in both views is the McIntire Building. It was constructed in 1911, after the Patterson Livery on the same site burned. (Leon Garrett photograph.)

To the right of the Presbyterian Church in this 1949 photograph is the massive Davenport Building, razed in the 1990s. Constructed in 1897 on the northwest corner of Tenth and State Streets, it housed storefronts and offices. Notable and surviving today is the Volunteer Fire Department Building at 1019 State Street. This building dates to before 1894, and this site was used for town council meetings and later served as the engine house for the volunteer fire department. (Leon Garrett photograph.)

A busy Main Street view from Center Street in 1949 shows the Central Hotel at right. Tucker Drugs is where the camera that took this photograph was purchased. Across the street, next to the Federal Building, was the Otho D. Porter Building, built in 1906. Porter was a prominent African American physician. Sadly, all buildings on the right in this photograph were razed by Bowling Green Municipal Utilities. Today the Warren County Regional Jail sits beside the Federal Building. (Leon Garrett photograph.)

In images from 1950 and 2009, changes along State Street are abundant. The view south from the Mariah Moore House in 1950 shows the impressive American Legion Post 23, originally the Carrie Burnam Taylor dressmaking facility. A busy street scene surrounds the massive Helm Hotel. Yellow Cab's sign is visible at right. Today the Helm location is occupied by U.S. Bank, and the attached garage sits on the site of the American Legion Hall. (Leon Garrett photograph.)

Views from the roof of the Citizen's National Bank, now U.S. Bank, show State Street looking north. Noticeable changes between 1972 and today are the remodeling of the Mariah Moore home into Mariah's 1818 restaurant and demolitions on the west side of State Street. Pace Service Company, Webb Chevrolet, and the State Motel are all missing from the 700 and 800 blocks of State Street. These locations are now vacant lots and Circus Square Park. (Marshall Love photograph.)

A 1948 photograph looking north on College Street from near Eleventh Street shows Bowling Green City Hall, at left, and the Diamond Theatre in the next block. The next year, the Diamond would be remodeled into the State Theatre, currently Fountain Square Church. Across the street are the Park Row Apartments, which replaced a building that had housed several businesses, including Guys and Dolls pool hall and, previously, a Goodyear service center. (Leon Garrett photograph.)

Contrasting images show College Street looking south toward Western Kentucky University's Cherry Hall on top of Western's Hill. In the 1948 view, Cumberland Presbyterian Church, used from 1909 until 1971, is visible at College and Eleventh Streets. A crossing guard helps children get to College Street Public School. In the 2009 view, the 15-story Bowling Green Towers and the English, Lucas, Priest, and Owsley Law Offices dominate. The church was replaced by Big B Cleaners. (Leon Garrett photograph.)

This Main Street view from Kentucky Street in 1949 shows multiple businesses occupying the south side of the 200 block. Looking east between Kentucky and Center Streets, Avery's Barber Shop, Hunt's Oyster Bar, several other structures, and the Federal Building are all visible. In the 2009 view, the Federal Building remains, but the Warren County Regional Jail has replaced eight buildings that fronted Main Street. The jail complex stretches up Kentucky Street two blocks to Eleventh Street. (Leon Garrett photograph.)

The north side of the 100 block of East Main Street, pictured in this view from the early 1960s, shows POWR-LITE Electric occupying the Potter House Hotel building. This edifice was also the home of Galvin's Grocery for 42 years until the 1920s. With the first L&N passenger stations nearby until 1925, this area thrived. Later in decay, most of this entire block was razed in the early 1990s for the Bowling Green Municipal Utilities Operations Center. (Marshall Love photograph.)

CHAPTER 3

FOUNTAIN SQUARE

This view of the Fountain Square Park is one of many featured on postcards. Bowling Green's central park remains a very popular subject, with many photographs taken here since 1900. The pictured scene of gentlemen sitting around the fountain is duplicated even today, as families enjoy visiting the park for relaxation, study, events, and photographs. (Greg Hughes collection.)

The only known photograph that shows the original fountain features the Gilbert Sisters Band performing in Fountain Square around 1871. Visible is Mallory Drugs in the Barclay Building, constructed before 1860. To the left of the Barclay Building is Emanuel Nahm Dry Goods. In the current photograph, note the newer Nahm Building constructed in 1888. The Barclay Building, longtime home of Rabold's Menswear, is one of few on Main Street to survive a Civil War fire. (Kentucky Library Collection, WKU.)

FOUNTAIN SQUARE

An early-1880s photograph of Park Row shows, at left, the building that eventually housed the original Citizen's National Bank, formed in 1901. At center is the Cooke Building, constructed around 1880 and housing the *Southern Progress* weekly newspaper. Note the fence around the park erected to keep livestock out. Today the Cooke Building is divided into two storefronts. The Odd Fellows Building is to the right, constructed in 1892 for I. B. Wilford. (Kentucky Library Collection, WKU.)

The northern entrance to Fountain Square Park features an arch carved from Warren County oolitic limestone from the Smallhouse Quarry. This arch was a gift to Bowling Green from Samuel Walker in May 1916. It was carved by W. W. Backus, who also carved the columns on the Warren County Courthouse. A similar arch was added to the Park Row entrance in December 1959. It honors Mayor C. W. Lampkin, who died in office, and his brother E. F. Lampkin. (Greg Hughes collection.)

Seen here in 1949, Park Row was once called "Frozen Row," because the weak winter sun rarely shines on it, keeping fallen snow around. At the end of the sidewalk, across College Street, is the H. A. McElroy dime store. It burned in 1950 and was replaced with a two-story version. To the right are three buildings erected in 1892—the Nolan, Daughtry, and Ackerman Buildings. Retailer J. C. Penney was in the Ackerman Building from 1925 to 1978. (Leon Garrett photograph.)

In 1972, the replica Eiffel Tower still stood in Fountain Square Park. A memorial to World War I veterans, it was moved in 1979 to Davis-Hoffman Veterans Cemetery, a part of Fairview Cemetery. The 2009 view is also missing Woolworth's dime store and the old Citizen's National Bank at the left, both razed in 1992. On the Cooke Building, the mural *Henri in Bowling Green*, by Andee Rudloff, was covered during construction of BB&T bank in 2009. (Marshall Love photograph.)

CHAPTER 4

BUSINESS AND INDUSTRY

Livery stables were once a common sight around Bowling Green. Besides boarding and grooming services, one could rent a horse and buggy or, in later years, even an automobile. Liveries also provided horse-drawn funeral coaches. Here workers proudly show their wares outside George Collet's Livery, later the site of the Federal Building on Main Street. (Marshall Love collection.)

This building at 1224 Indianola Street was constructed in 1890 and was once the home of Bowling Green's oldest manufacturing company. The H. B. Scott Tobacco Company formed in 1900 and produced 19 brands of chewing tobacco, rolled into twists. Their Warren County Twist won a gold medal at the 1904 St. Louis World's Fair. Scott Tobacco moved to Adams Street in 1939. Now covered in siding, this building is occupied by Flooring Hub, a flooring business. (Kentucky Library Collection, WKU.)

Between 1927 and 1975, the Pet Milk Company operated near the lower end of Church Street. Milk production was high in Warren County for many years, and the plant was very successful. The L&N Portage Railroad passed behind the rear of the property, which assisted in the shipping operations. Today a portion of the building is used as warehouse space. The lower Church Street industrial area has largely been forgotten. At one time, many industries operated here. (Kentucky Library Collection, WKU.)

The Spot Cash Store has been in continuous operation here since January 1929. Three generations of the Davis family have run the store. Long ago, it was the home of Newton's Restaurant. Other enterprises to occupy this building were Compton and O'Bryan Saloon, Hale and Wilson Store, and Roy McCormack Billiards. The older image was taken prior to 1903, when the Slade Building at right was rebuilt as the Patsy Fitzpatrick Building, with a concrete facade added by Fitzpatrick. (Marshall Love collection.)

One of the best-known businesses in Bowling Green is the Carpenter-Dent-Sublett Drug Stores chain. C.D.S. No. 4, shown here in 1949, was one of several drugstores downtown. From 1912 until 1928, the Willis Drug Store operated here prior to being purchased by C.D.S. C.D.S. No. 10 on Ashley Circle is the only one still in operation in Bowling Green. Longtime neighbor United Furniture now occupies most of the Price Building. (Leon Garrett photograph.)

The Potter-Matlock Bank was erected on this site in 1906. Following a merger with American National Bank in 1958, the facade was changed, and this later steel-and-glass structure replaced the fronts of the original Potter-Matlock building and others. The original Seth Thomas clock was moved here in the 1940s from Campbell Jewelers. Destroyed during an automobile accident in 1974, it was replaced in 1976. National City Bank is now part of PNC Bank. (Greg Hughes collection.)

BUSINESS AND INDUSTRY

John C. Gerard first established an undertaking business in Bowling Green in 1843. The business passed through many generations of the Gerard family. The older image shows a horse-drawn hearse on the dusty streets of the city. The longtime business home at Tenth and College Streets, previously Court and Summer Streets, remains remarkably unchanged. The 2009 view shows it as the Robertson Building, housing the Bratcher law firm. (Kentucky Library Collection, WKU.)

Sam Pushin had sold dry goods since the 1890s and needed a larger space for his growing business. Designed by Creedmore Fleenor, this large structure opened in 1921 at Main and College Streets. A rear addition was later built. After Pushin's closed in 1980, it became an office building. Now an art studio and Corsair Artisian Distillery operate from the rear portion of the building on Fountain Square. (Leon Garrett photograph.)

In 1877, James Woolworth established an axe-handle factory in Bowling Green. This was one of the city's early industries. The company merged with the Turner-Day Company in 1884 and became the largest manufacturer of hickory striking-tool handles. Turner-Day-Woolworth was acquired by True Temper Corporation in 1951. Today the main building survives as Causey's Collision Center. The old Portage Railroad tracks are gone, but the right-of-way is still visible. (Kentucky Library Collection, WKU.)

J. C. Kirby started in the funeral business in 1947. In 1962, Kirby and Carleen Goodrum purchased the Cliff Raymer Funeral Home at 832 Broadway. A year later, Kirby and Goodrum became J. C. Kirby and Son. Since 1987, the business has been owned by son Kevin Kirby. At one time, ambulance services were provided to the area by local funeral homes. This building has been remodeled some 27 times and has also served as the county coroner's office. (Marshall Love photograph.)

The older photograph shows a packed Plaza Shopping Center during a promotional event in 1962. In 1959, Bowling Green's first strip mall had opened with a Ben Franklin five-and-dime store as an anchor, along with a pharmacy, hardware store, fashion clothing store, and laundry The newer view shows the final days of Houchen's Market as the anchor, but the center is still home to Dollar General Stores and the Wishy Washy coin-operated laundry. (Marshall Love photograph.)

Worthy of restoration, the Honey Krust Bakery sits at 1349 Adams Street. Local architect James Ingram was the award-winning designer of this building in 1936. The bakery operated here into the 1980s as Honey Krust, Kern's, Colonial, Sunbeam, and other brands. At one time, the bakery served a 60-mile radius with 15 trucks. Now the building is partially used for a garage and has decayed extensively. The adjoining Hostess House is now used as rental property. (Kentucky Library Collection, WKU.)

In May 1940, Union Underwear broke ground on Bowling Green's first major manufacturing facility at 700 Church Street. Six hundred sewing machines were operated, mainly by women. During World War II, the operation provided underwear for American servicemen. Fruit of the Loom maintains its international headquarters in Bowling Green. The original plant is now headquarters for Houchen's Industries. Started as a rural grocery, Houchen's has grown to include marketing, financial, trucking, grocery, warehousing, construction, recycling, and insurance businesses. (Leon Garrett photograph.)

Leon Garrett ran this radio shop at 425 East Seventh Street between 1952 and 1955. Today this area is the site of the Bowling Green Area Chamber of Commerce at Seventh and College Streets. Across Seventh Street, the Standard Oil station has been restored as restrooms for Circus Square Park. The park features an interactive fountain, hosts concerts and events, and takes up an entire city block. Across College Street, the Southern Kentucky Performing Arts Center is under construction. (Leon Garrett photograph.)

CHAPTER 5

TRANSPORTATION

This second Bowling Green Depot was a cigar-shaped structure set amid several tracks between Adams and Clay Streets at Main Street. It had replaced the depot burned during the Civil War.

Across Adams Street was the large Rauscher House Hotel. The popular 45-room hotel suffered after the new L&N Depot was opened a few blocks north in 1925. (Greg Hughes collection.)

The boat landing played an important role in Bowling Green's development. For many years, boats arrived carrying passengers and freight into the city, and the Bowling Green and Evansville Packet Company operated here for nearly 100 years. The Portage Railroad moved the freight from boats and warehouses to the downtown area. This view shows the steamer *Chaperon* and barges of asphalt. Today this spot is relegated to recreational fishing and boating on the scenic Barren River. (Marshall Love collection.)

The L&N Railroad maintained a busy yard stretching between Fourth and Tenth Streets in Bowling Green for more than 100 years until moving 5 miles south to Memphis Junction in the late 1970s. The 1949 view shows a steam engine working the yard and the L&N Freight Depot at Main and Adams Streets. Today CSX operates the Main Line Subdivision between Louisville and Nashville. The tractor dealership building survived several uses until purchased and razed by Bowling Green Municipal Utilities. (Leon Garrett photograph.)

On February 15, 1921, Louisville and Nashville freight No. 74 derailed eight cars on the Barren River Bridge. Overnight, crews worked to salvage materials from the cars, with pieces of wrecked cars and contents dumped in the river. On February 16, as spectators gathered, some bridge girders were dynamited. During the explosion, Dan Cornwell, a carpenter, was struck in the head and killed by debris. The current bridge, owned by L&N successor CSX, carries several trains each day. (Marshall Love collection.)

The Bowling Green–Warren County Airport began hosting local pilots and a flying school in 1934. This view from August 1948 shows the terminal building on the first day of Eastern Airlines interstate service. Thousands attended the event, which included a military air show. Eastern eventually provided four daily flights but later scaled back service, which was discontinued in 1972. Today there is no flight control center, and most traffic consists of local pilots and refueling stops. (Leon Garrett photograph.)

In 1940, Duncan Hines moved his home and office to this 4-acre lot north of Bowling Green on Louisville Road. In his years here, the estate boasted gardens and orchards, and Hines continued to produce his restaurant guide *Adventures in Good Eating*. His guides helped people find good food and lodging while traveling. After his death in 1959, the Hardy family moved its funeral business here in 1960, expanding the funeral home to its present size. (Kentucky Library Collection, WKU.)

A significant change to Bowling Green's downtown area took place upon the completion of the 31W Bypass around the eastern part of the city in 1949. While this relieved traffic congestion in the business district, it also took patrons away to the new route. Travelers had many new options for gasoline, lodging, dining, and shopping. As the city has stretched past Interstate 65, hundreds of new businesses have opened on Scottsville Road and Campbell Lane. (Marshall Love photograph.)

Professional baseball in Bowling Green had been played during the 1940s by the Barons of the Kentucky-Illinois-Tennessee or Kitty League. Games were played at the Fairgrounds, near where Lehman Avenue intersects the 31W Bypass today. The Class A Bowling Green Hot Rods of the South Atlantic League drew 232,987 to Bowling Green Ballpark in their inaugural season of 2009. A DX gas station once operated at the corner of Eighth and Kentucky Streets, shown in a 1950s photograph. (Marshall Love photograph.)

In the 1920s, the Firestone Tire Company opened service centers around the country. The Bowling Green location on Broadway has been open since 1958. The store originally sold gasoline, tires, and even refrigerators. A retread center adjoined in the same building, and that portion houses Grandma's Attic consignment today. The Firestone business remains successful as a busy repair center and tire showroom. It is the oldest surviving service center in the Nashville region. (Leon Garrett photograph.)

Lost River Cave has been the site of Confederate and Union army camps, a Jesse James hideout, milling operations, and cave tours. An underground "Nite Club" was operated between 1933 and 1960. Afterward, the area became a dump. Thanks to the Friends of Lost River and WKU, it has made a grand comeback as one of Bowling Green's most popular tourist attractions. Thousands of visitors now tour the Lost River Cave and Valley each year. (Greg Hughes collection.)

EDUCATION AND RELIGION

Ogden College was founded in 1877 through a gift from Robert Ogden to provide secondary education to young men from Warren County. The building, constructed as the Thomas Calvert residence around 1870, had become a school before completion. As part of WKU in the late 1960s, it was razed to build the central wing of Thompson Complex. (Greg Hughes collection.)

Henry Hardin Cherry Hall was opened for classes in September 1937. The building's namesake had passed away in August of the same year. That November, a statue of Dr. Cherry was erected in front. The Brinton B. Davis–designed building at the top of Vinegar Hill at Fifteenth and College Streets housed 50 classrooms, 16 labs, 60 offices, the bookstore, and a post office when it opened. Today it houses the English, history, religion, and philosophy departments for WKU. (Leon Garrett photograph.)

EDUCATION AND RELIGION

The Towers was constructed in 1901 after fire destroyed the old Southern Normal School in 1899. The 1852 Atwood Hobson mansion had become a school after the Hobsons moved to their Riverview home. Southern Normal moved up the hill, eventually becoming Western Kentucky University. The Business University occupied the Towers until merging with WKU in 1963. Known as "The Castle," it burned in 1964 and was replaced with the 15-story Bowling Green Towers at 1149 College Street. (Marshall Love collection.)

College Street School opened in 1882 and was the first graded public school in Bowling Green. This three-story structure was remembered by former students for the circular fire escape and the fact that the only restrooms were on the first floor. The large school was razed in 1961 for the construction of a new U.S. Post Office, which faces Eleventh Street today. The post office moved to this location from the Federal Building. (Kentucky Library Collection, WKU.)

Bowling Green High School was built on Center Street in 1923. The Junior High School at right was built in 1929. The high school moved to Rockingham Lane in 1970, leaving the junior high to use the entire complex until moving in 2001. Views from 1950 and today will sadden those who attended school here. A developer has gutted the schools' interiors, including the adjoining gymnasium, to create apartment buildings that remain unfinished after several years. (Leon Garrett photograph.)

Dating to 1833, The Presbyterian Church on the southwest corner of State and Tenth Streets is one of Bowling Green's landmark structures. The church survived the Civil War as a Union hospital and an 1895 fire in the steeple. An expansion to the left in the 1940s took the place of the mid-19th-century Warren County Jail, while expansion to the rear in the 1990s necessitated the razing of the Cooke Building, which housed professional offices. (Kentucky Library Collection, WKU.)

Center Street Public School opened in 1908 and featured two and a half stories and a basement. Later the school expanded into the Bible Presbyterian Church building next door. The large school building and the addition were both razed in 1962. Bowling Green's daily newspaper dates to the mid-1800s and has grown to serve a six-county region. A large printing plant for the *Park City Daily News* replaced some retail buildings on this site. (Kentucky Library Collection, WKU.)

State Street Methodist Church at 1101 State Street was constructed in 1895. Built of Bowling Green limestone, it contained 77 stained-glass windows and features a five-story bell tower. Methodists organized in Bowling Green in 1819, split into north-south factions over slavery and state's rights in 1844, and eventually reunited in 1939. The view from a 1940s postcard shows the original entrance, while the current view reflects the entrance created during a 1950s renovation. (Greg Hughes collection.)

ate Street Methodist Church-Bowling Green, Ky.

3-A-15

State Street Baptist Church was established in 1838 from the slave membership of First Baptist Church, becoming the first organized church for African Americans in Bowling Green. On May 4, 2000, during roof replacement, a worker's torch ignited a blaze that destroyed the roof and much of the interior of the 100-year-old structure. Fortunately, the church was rebuilt using the original walls. Today State Street Baptist Church is the anchor of the Shake Rag Historic District. (Ben Runner Jr. photograph.)

Westminster Presbyterian Church was constructed on the corner of State and Twelfth Streets in 1912 and features Bowling Green limestone. This congregation of Westminster Presbyterian Church moved here from its previous location at the corner of Center and Eleventh Streets and remained here until reuniting with The Presbyterian Church at Tenth and State Streets in 1949. Today this building houses Victory Baptist Church and still features the original temple front, stained-glass windows, and cast-iron dome. (Greg Hughes collection.)

CHAPTER

ENTERTAINMENT AND RECREATION

This 1930s photograph shows Love's Links, a short-lived miniature golf course operated by entrepreneur Marshall Love Sr. on Tenth Street across from the Denhardt Armory. A fine Bowling Green photographer, Marshall Love Jr. contributed many of the images in this book. He ran Love's Studio on Laurel Avenue from 1958 until his retirement in 1990. (Marshall Love collection.)

87

The Ogden Building on the northwest corner of Main and State Streets was constructed around 1870 and replaced the two-story 1820s Washington Hall hotel, which burned during the Civil War. Pictured here in 1911, the building was occupied by the 200-seat Elite Theatre, a motion picture house. Later this was home to Nell O'Bryan's hat shop, Willoughby Grocery, and Carpenter-Dent-Sublett Drugstore No. 6. Current occupant Hilliard Lyons renovated the building in 1981. (Marshall Love collection.)

ELITE THEATRE BOWLING GREEN, KY. OCT. 16, 1911

The Riverside Drive-In Theatre opened June 27, 1950, showing *Boy from Indiana*. Adult admission was 45¢, with children under 12 admitted free. Providing entertainment for many years, the Riverside finally closed in August 1985, leaving Bowling Green without a drive-in theater. After deteriorating for nearly 10 years, it was razed in May 1995 to make room for Riverside Center, containing a large Kroger grocery and other shops. The older view is from Thanksgiving 1994. (Ben Runner Jr. photograph.)

Roach Radio and Television was started by Browder Roach in 1938 in an old gas station building on College Street. By 1955, Roach had moved to the building shown here and added a showroom to the front. This is typical of several downtown businesses occupying former private residences. One of the first places in Bowling Green to offer color television sets, Roach Radio and Television lasted until Roach's retirement in the 1970s. Today it is the home of Quality Awning Company. (Leon Garrett photograph.)

Radio Station WLBJ opened at the junction of Lehman and Fairview Avenues in June 1940 featuring local programming. At the time, it was at the northeast edge of Bowling Green near the fairgrounds. In 1961, the station moved farther out Cemetery Road near Indian Hills, and it remained there until signing off for good in 1991. With the top portion still visible, the original building today stands in the middle of Johnson-Vaughn-Phelps funeral home. (Kentucky Library Collection, WKU.)

The 726-seat Princess Theatre opened in 1914 and is believed to have been the first motion picture theater in Kentucky to have sound. It closed in 1957 and was converted to retail space. The seating area was demolished, and the front of the building was covered with siding. Today the marquee is gone, and the building houses Alan Davis photography at 432 East Main Street. To the right of Alan Davis photography, the Johnson Building, constructed in 1935, has housed Golden-Farley since 1959. (Leon Garrett photograph.)

Charles Ray Woosley and his family purchased Murray's Restaurant on the northeast corner of Eighth and College Streets in the early 1960s, opening Ray's Hamburgers. With the 31W Bypass pulling traffic away from downtown, Woosley opened Ray's Drive-In on the 31W Bypass near Riverside Drive-In Theatre. He also became one of the first Kentucky Fried Chicken franchisees and later had a successful catering business. Today Advance Auto Parts occupies the site. (Judy Woosley collection.)

Jonesville was an African American community formed after the Civil War between the L&N Railroad, Dogwood Drive, and Russellville Road. The area grew to become home to a few hundred residents, Mount Zion Baptist Church, Jonesville Elementary School, and businesses. Targeted for urban renewal, the land was acquired by the state and sold to Western Kentucky University in the 1960s. E. A. Diddle Arena, Houchens-Smith Stadium, Nick Denes Field, Supply-Services Building, and University Boulevard occupy this site today. (Marshall Love photograph.)

ENTERTAINMENT AND RECREATION

Leon Garrett was not quite 21 years old and a student at Western Kentucky State College when he was photographed during spring 1949. A huge Hilltopper fan then and now, Garrett was also quite the shutterbug. Many of the photographs in this book were taken by him between 1948 and 1950 with his Argus C3 camera. Away from Bowling Green for many years and now retired, Garrett has returned home, where he can again follow WKU sports. (Leon Garrett photograph.)

www.arcadiapublishing.com

Discover books about the town where you grew up, the cities where your friends and families live, the town where your parents met, or even that retirement spot you've been dreaming about. Our Web site provides history lovers with exclusive deals, advanced notification about new titles, e-mail alerts of author events, and much more.

MADE IN THE **USA**

Arcadia Publishing, the leading local history publisher in the United States, is committed to making history accessible and meaningful through publishing books that celebrate and preserve the heritage of America's people and places. Consistent with our mission to preserve history on a local level, this book was printed in South Carolina on American-made paper and manufactured entirely in the United States.

This book carries the accredited Forest Stewardship Council (FSC) label and is printed on 100 percent FSC-certified paper. Products carrying the FSC label are independently certified to assure consumers that they come from forests that are managed to meet the social, economic, and ecological needs of present and future generations.

FSC
Mixed Sources
Product group from well-managed
forests and other controlled sources

Cert no. SW-COC-001530
www.fsc.org
© 1996 Forest Stewardship Council

Find Your Place in History.